THE RAIN BARREL

THE RAIN BARREL
FRANK ORMSBY

WAKE
FOREST
UNIVERSITY
PRESS

First North American edition

© Frank Ormsby, 2019

For permission, write to
Wake Forest University Press
Post Office Box 7333
Winston-Salem, NC 27109
wfupress.wfu.edu
wfupress@wfu.edu

ISBN 978-1-930630-89-5 (paperback)

Library of Congress Control Number 2018965398

Designed and typeset by
Nathan Moehlmann, Goosepen Studio & Press.

First published in the USA by Wake Forest University Press in 2020
under license from Bloodaxe Books Ltd.
First published in the UK in 2019 by Bloodaxe Books Ltd.

Publication of this book was generously supported by the Boyle Family Fund.

for Ciaran and Deirdre Carson

CONTENTS

Beyond the Walls

THE RAIN BARREL

UNTROUBLED

Caesar is flattening Gaul
by the light of our Tilley.
My father has slept
with his mouth open
since the beginning of the war.
My mother is on a cleaning campaign
in the furthest corners of her empire.
The frozen center of the night
is a dog's yowl released between hills.
I am translating from the Latin.
It is 1962, JFK smiles from our mantelpiece.
Before the decade is out
we will fear the unmarked car in the lay-by,
the live device thrown into the garden.
But on this quiet night
logs are burning out in the stove
and a dog in the hills
is fashioning a winter elegy.

THE BLACK KETTLE

Now that the new stove is in place and throwing its heat
the full length of the kitchen,
we have replaced the black kettle.
It no longer hangs over the open fire
on a lethal hook like a piece of dungeon furniture.
I want to angle it at the front door, fill it with clay
and seed it with snowdrops and primroses.

Or better still,
we could cultivate something scarlet and spreading,
a nasturtium, say,
with a statement to make about color.
Saved from a rusty nail in the barn,
its colors doubled, the kettle would bed in
as though it had always been there,
at home and visible and unmistakably ours;
a local fire-god with a tongue of flowers.

THE BEEKEEPER

The Captain's wife keeps bees in a walled orchard.
Dressed like a tiny astronaut, she leans
into the raw engine of the hive. The fury of the bees
seems nothing to her. She takes the stings
and goes forward without fear.
The whole afternoon is rich in appetites and satisfactions.
The bees that have sucked from the juice
of the fallen apples, lie sozzled under the trees.

FUCHSIA

The earrings, the lanterns, the tassels
of the fuchsia change before our eyes.
Now they are bells, now frozen tears,
now blood-drops from the heart of summer.
The fuchsia hedge is redolent of old battles,
a peaceful tapestry in the annals of stone.

THE WILD DOG ROSE

Planted by our neighbor when she first came here
—frail stems, anaemic petals—it was dying from the start.
A watercolor among flowers, it rose from its bed by the door
with a pale hospitality. It, too,
needed shelter from the wind that one day soon
would leave it in tatters. Always as she approached the door,
our neighbor bent to touch the tallest flower.
"It's only me," she murmured. "I won't stay long."

FOXGLOVES

Nothing more lovely than the speckled throat
of the foxglove, or its pinks and purples and reds
inflaming the hedges. It seems to renew
all colors and wear them like the fabrics of African women.
So versatile they might poison you
or do your heart good, the foxgloves are imperious
around the farm. Cowslips and buttercups
will never aspire to the belled heights of the foxglove
or be photographed decorously among the wheelchairs
of a chapel hospital, or spotlessly aproned at a stall
for the needy. Mostly we relished their assonantal sound
and avoided their stain. They dwelt and flowered
in the margin, bent towards us just enough to be admired,
holding their maverick selves up to the sun
between the snapdragon and the wild dog rose,
between the green briars and the rhododendrons.

THE BUTTERFLY HOUSE

One more butterfly in the butterfly house
will count as overcrowding. Sun all morning
and the heaviness of piped heat
draws hundreds to the surface. They spend their days

being exquisite in a history without wars. We are able,
briefly, to forget the scaly intent,
the cold-skinned slither a hundred yards away
in the tropical ravine. Hold up your arm

and with luck you will emerge into the garden,
badged and sleeved with butterflies,
a thousand bright sails opening around you.

ROMAN LAUREL

In the gardens of the upwardly mobile,
in the official dark greenery of municipal shrubs,
at roundabouts, under shadowy memorials,
look to find, especially at night,
when it takes its sheen from lofty streetlamps
and the seasonal moon,
the decorous hide-and-seek
of the Roman Laurel.

COWS (1)

Their eyes are innocence
peeled back to its limits,
still wet from the Creation.

COWS (2)

The utter ignominy
of being ignored by cattle.
Instantly you become
the chomping sound between their jaws.
You might as well have disappeared
into the Witness Protection Program,
unless a gate lies open
from one field to another,
unless the farm boy comes to gather
the cows for the night
and calls them vigorously by name.

COWS (3)

We never got used to cows,
the oddness of the odd
inhabiting our fields...
their big grass-junkie eyes,
their unfortunate lugs,
their bottom-of-the-class stare,
the amiable, ambling afterthought
of their progress round the farm,
their languid tail-work,
the way they could shit on the move.
Days ended with the pageantry of cows
herded out of sunset and into byres.
Somewhere in their bovinity they too
seemed curious about us —
the humans who worked the milking machines
and drove the tractors
and spoke an incomprehensible language.
How odd we must have seemed
in our rubber boots
and plastic man-gear. Not a tail among us.

AT THE ELVIS CONVENTION

1

The Ballygawley Elvis strutted, chest exposed,
in white bell-bottoms. Practice curls of the lip
from the Omagh Elvis and a handful of diaphanous scarves
to be thrown into the crowd.
The Bundoran Elvis managed so much droop
on his lopsided smile, he appeared to be having a stroke.
Everyone was in a Vegas frame of mind,
rhinestones fingered as though they were rosary beads.

2

Three hours later I sat with the disappointed,
their makeup beginning to run.
Slowly they circled back to themselves,
morose, deflated and less than they had been.
Forty years an Elvis, one lamented, and nothing to show.
Already it was too late. Young hip-swingers were coming through
in Carrickmacross and Caledon and Donegal Town,
sounding more like the real thing than the real thing.
His sunglasses, his glossy sideburns would all go to waste,
unless he could reinvent himself, as Engelbert Humperdinck for example,
or Roy Orbison or Johnny Cash. Who would want to be himself
any longer than he had to?
"*Mercy*," he growls into an imaginary mic,
then plays the opening chords of "Pretty Woman"
like a man who has been practicing.

THE SOUND OF TRAINS

New York

The trains have a different rush and a different cry
in the gully behind the houses.
Sometimes, heard from a distance, they are the sound
of a Manhattan summer, boiling in the sun.
Closer, a cemetery runs beside them for miles.
Here they utter their redemptive holler,
as though the Angel Gabriel were on board,
as though they had shaped a special cry to greet
a field of tombstones. Sometimes, in the small hours,
they are a flute tuning up, or a harmonica's opening
wail, but they never get beyond the first note
of their threnody for bruised spirits,
a drawn-out blues, as I imagine it, that picks up words
in boxcars among the hoboes, and in the long trains
that take an age to worm out of town. They arouse the dark
more than the ticking lust of cicadas. Alone at our windows,
or blessed with company, we will never get used to the trains'
faint undercurrent of alarm, the way each leaves,
briefly, in the air, its different rush and cry,
how each, with its hoarse flair and yearning fall,
announces its passing.

SEASIDE

1

We think of it as a big lake in the Free State
that is somehow attached to trains.
Bernie McMulkin says
you can smell the sea before you see it. It's over there!
It's over there where the seagulls are diving.
Already, we have broken
into a run, but cannot yet
take the sea in our stride.
We make frantic swimming motions in the air.

2

As usual Da is the one who volunteers
to be buried. We dig his grave
at the edge of the beach and tuck him in
until only his head is visible.
The wind blows sand in his eyes but the tide
is hours away, and miles away the cold
shadow of the mountain.

THE DISAPPEARED

There are lost graves on the mountain
but somebody knows where they are:
the man with the cleanest boots in town,
the man with the spotless car.

TODAY THERE HAS
BEEN INFORMATION

Today there has been information and it is time again
to ransack the mountain. His mother has hired a psychic
and the slow searcher's walk continues into its tenth year.
The mother, as always, carries the photograph of her son
in the tilted boater. He might be about to tip the hat
and bid us good morrow. Or has he been snapped
in the chorus line of, say, a musical?
Despite his showbiz air, he is not smiling.
Even without hindsight, we would register his anxiety.
Nine years have passed and today there has been
information. The search parties re-form.
Hope trickles again like a mountain stream
they must follow to its source. They search every dip
in the heather, consult their notes
about flooded hollows and rocks and nameless bushes,
the hundred anonymous landmarks in a bland landscape
that has changed with the seasons.
It has been nine years and the voice on the telephone
was uncertain and the police are again pressing for information.

DAWN CHORUS,
WITH PAINTING BY JOAN MIRÓ

On my birthday I walk barefoot, downstairs
and find your card, *The Singer* by Joan Miró, propped on the mantelpiece.
Already the day promises music, already I catch
the opening imperatives of the dawn chorus,
an avant-garde concert to rouse the neighborhood.
The blackbird takes it away, spontaneously joyful,
and soon the trees are ringing with brilliant originals,
clear notes and high-pitched harmonies.
Looped and lassoed, I follow, as far as I can, their mazy tangles,
strings and laces of sound.
Now the chorus has moved on, perhaps to embrace the males'
potency and gift for mating, the musical strut
of those randy, commanding little gods.
Then the virtuoso stuff, motifs and riffs
and effortless duets. You want to stand and applaud
or imagine a myth for the minstrels of the dawn
to make sense of their history.
This morning, again, it is possible to believe
that joy grows irresistibly at the roots of everything,
close to that fissure in Chaos,
where the birds erupted through the last freezing tunnel
from Eden. Their memories were mostly of music,
but they carried also a protective panic
that still shivers when we approach and linger.
How young are these old masters who endlessly renew
their dialogue with the air? In Miró's painting
homage takes the form of the men's bird-like features —
the open beaks, the big bird's-eye-shape on the vocalist's face.

The microphones are primed, the band looks drunk
on bubbly and in the mood to improvise.
The birds, so far as we can tell, may be polishing their grace notes
or sharpening the throat-needles of song that skewer our attention.
They might be taking time out from a champagne breakfast,
or a garden party. So the day becomes more than a birthday,
as pure birdsong lifts from the trees and Miró's band
tunes up for a lively session. If I write under your name
that it is good to be alive, I hope you won't think it
a failure of sentiment, surrounded as I am
by such artistries of color and sound.
Whatever the day brings, it will retain
this morning's ripe underswell, its ageless echo.

TOWARDS AN ELEGY

If I should write your elegy,
it would be when December light
darkens the windows.
Watching light fall
on the black rocks in the bay,
the disused lighthouse
where you lived,
the green headland
where no ship ever foundered,
would be a mode
of getting used to your death.
I've been assembling you from notes…
your love of the natural world,
your tastes in music,
that line from "Dover Beach"
where a light gleams on the French coast
and is gone. I smile to think of you,
a serious man
debating how best to live.
Should you retreat
into your lighthouse
and bar the door,
or throw the door open
from time to time,
a gregarious recluse?
How could I catch the way
your small talk turned in passing
into something large?
Once, meeting me on the stairs, you remarked:

"All laughter is sycophantic."
(I didn't laugh for days after that.)
It would be a tough assignment, friend,
to produce a life impression
neither reduced nor diminished.
May the dawn not find me here,
still gazing out to sea,
the tide swarming over the mudflats,
the page still blank
but for the first line, perhaps,
"If I should write your elegy,"
and the last:
"You gleamed and are gone."

SMALL THINGS

When I remarked to the two old boys in the park
that I had not glimpsed the heron lately,
they were beside themselves with disappointment:
"You missed him by five minutes. He flew across to the island."
They cast about for fitting consolation.
"Have you seen the egrets?" I had not. "There's two of them
lives in the Milewater Stream. Keep an eye out for them."
That's three pleasures: the old boys
in their baseball caps delighting in small things,
the small things made precious by their delight,
to everyone who will listen, which today,
in this stretch of the park, is everyone.

SMALL WORLD (4)

I set my cap
at a rakish angle.
Autumn breezes into town.

*

In your hair, scents of autumn.
Only by embracing
can I be sure.

*

Belfast Lough
swashbuckles ashore,
a love child of the grey Atlantic.

*

Summer surrenders.
Autumn, the lovely destroyer,
heads for the trees.

*

Old friends at the tavern.
A mile home in the dark
as the cow flees.

*

Fooled into flower
by an early spring,
the daffodils die.

*

A hermit bird, the corncrake.
With each spare cry
he breaks a vow of silence.

*

The heron fluffs
his landing. A straight face
from every fowl on the lake.

*

Wind across bogland,
a melancholy score
for corncrake, snipe, curlew.

*

Ochone! Ochone!
Now that the corncrake's back,
we can be our plaintive selves.

FROM *A BELFAST JOURNAL*

Ashes of half-soles and stiletto heels,
       the blacks and blues
of straps and smoldering uppers;
       I am burning old shoes
on a bonfire in the garden,
       some of them yours:
everyday wear, the ornate, sad
       debris of the dancing years,
and bedroom slippers long trodden out of shape,
       going up in smoke
with ancient, springless chairs that were not ours.
       The card table someone broke
before we came here, tea chests full of straw,
       they are acrid with the lives
that came to discard them,
       combustible as dead leaves.
No longer is it possible to tell
       which pairs we wore
walking at sunset in a loughside field
       that summer before
we traveled to terraces and pavement trees;
       or which embedded
the flattened pebbles of a country road,
       the grit that ached and faded
to less than pain or pearl of memory.
       Perhaps these helped to bear
the child inside you later when we trudged
       from one street to another with kitchenware
in suitcases and unpacked in larger rooms.

We might have piled
our first bonfire then — the books you claimed
            had come between us — pulled
pages from spines, the bookshelf from the wall —
            except that we knew nothing is solved
so simply. So I am burning our old shoes
            eleven years on and we are still involved
in calms and crises, manageable flux,
            contentment and pleasure.
This task is neither sentimental rite
            nor tedious chore; confidently insecure
I watch the dusty leather bubble and crack
            the flames working
in grace and anger and flickering perfection
            towards garden earth, dark ashes in a ring.

SAYING GOODBYE TO THE FAMILY

She sits in Departures with their children.
For the third time the passengers are asked
whether anyone has helped them pack
or added items to their luggage.
It's only this once, her husband explains patiently,
that he will, for business reasons, travel alone.
He hugs his children. His last presents to his wife
are a box of her favorite chocolates
and, deep in her suitcase, that delicate mechanism
of which she has no knowledge,
tick-tocking already towards the numbers in red.

WHITE-THROATED SPARROWS

The minute we stop to listen
the evening includes
us and the white-throated birds.
Sweetness and desire never set in words
inform the air, shape our most delicate moods.

THE LOVE POEM

Now that the love poem has been discredited,
and the language of tenderness is suspect,
and a day has been set aside for the shredding of the English love sonnet,
and praise of your eyes is condemned as fetishistic,
and words for your superlative ass are deemed inappropriate,
and endearments are piled on a bonfire,
and I'm frowned upon for a vocabulary that fondles
your peerless breasts, your exquisite streamlined feet.
Samizdat baby, my prohibition love,
aroused, we will melt underground, hire a room
out of sight, out of earshot, and devise new loving.
It will be the old loving, toughened and tenderized
by exile, rediscovered and passionate
on the fingertips and tongues of beginners and pioneers.
Later, granted the freedom of the city, elated,
we will emerge into the sunlight, the love poem reinstated.

CONVALESCENCE

If you slow down first, I shall slow down with you.
We will watch the fishermen unhook their catch.
When you stop, you will stamp your boots in the snow.
Under the maple tree, we'll find every leaf a collector's item.
We shall give my walking stick a dog's name.

THE BOOKMARK

When I open Thomas Hardy's *Selected Poems*,
randomly, between "The Oxen"and "Men Who March Away,"
I do not expect to loosen the dry repose
of a fossilized earwig, so browned and flattened
you could not name the decade
when somebody closed the book on him.

Beloved Hardy! But the next five minutes belong
to an earwig crushed to death in a book of poems,
the shape of its legs preserved in the dark stain.
I take mock-seriously a duty to preside
at its powdery exhumation, then choose the fire
in the library stove for its flare into nothingness.
Sentiment satisfied, obsequies observed,
I return Hardy, upright, to his place on the shelves.

SECONDHAND

1. The Secondhand Bookshop
for Mary Denvir

Once more I step into the afterlife
of secondhand books, the tunnels
where new dust accrues and different shelves
absorb the lighting. Mild foxing.
Perfect binding. I relish the wear and tear,
from the window display
angled away from the sun
to the untidy back room
like a fingerprint museum.
They pass through our hands
as a kind of seasoning,
ripen into the autumn and winter of books.

2. The Secondhand Book

Forgive me, whoever you are,
who pasted the dry leaf
into the inside back cover
and filled the spaces
around it with fragile endearments.
Forgive me! How tentatively
I have come to own
part of your unhappiness.

NITS

If there was an outbreak at school, it was not our fault.
One night a week the table was commandeered
for the Ministry of Nit Control. A fine comb steeped
in oil and drawn through the hair capsized
the nits onto the back page of the *Irish News*.
They were dead between two fingernails
before they could right themselves.
Now we were cleaner than a nurse's hands,
fresher than the soul after Confession,
though we spent half the morning
controlling the urge to scratch.

PRELIMINARIES

Early September, the ritual of backing the books.
As usual, the Taggarts are showing off,
their covers embossed wallpaper.
Others favor oilcloth or brown wrapping
or the sports pages from the *Irish News*.
On mine Rinty Monaghan and Spider Kelly
are striking a mean pose behind their gloves.
It is as if we have been let loose
for the year on flimsy orange jotters
with no upside-down, or exercise books
with our names pasted on the front.
The timetable with the colored squares
maps our tutelage:
nature study, potato cuts, catechism,
mathematics, geography, silent reading.

EVENING ON THE FARM:
EARLY WINTER

1

We are colder than we let on.
The moon is out early.
There's a gate into a snowy field
and beyond that a farmhouse
with lights in the yard
and just enough snow on the roof.
Every breath, animal and human,
is smoke on the lips.

2

We will have to be chased indoors,
or we'll build a snowman now,
in the dark, at the center of a field,
just to find him at dawn, dew-wet and sparkling,
while his face folds and his stomach liquefies.

POEM BEGINNING AND ENDING
WITH A DRUNKEN POET

Tang Dynasty

Snowflakes are melting into wine.
The poet, Li Po, drunk as a lord, has dropped his cap
in the dust and the way it blows back and forth
is the funniest thing he has ever seen.
Miss Wu fluffs a note from time to time
to attract the glance of her teacher
and again my heart aches for the poor scholar
catching fireflies to give himself light.
I wonder if the dead who roam T'ai Mountain
are visible tonight or indistinguishable from the mist.
But here comes the poet Meng Jiao
with a supply of chrysanthemum home brew,
getting tipsy on the taste of autumn.

THE POETS

The Poets are spaced out singly
around the park in dark overcoats.
Even the women are wearing bowlers.
Deaf to the barbarous vowels of the waterfowl,
they talk to themselves
in an elegant, indecipherable murmur,
unnerving the swans.

These are the famous poets. We have heard them praised
for their cryptic style and the music of their utterance,
though what we might say to them or they to us
is still a mystery. Even as I watch, they begin to levitate.
Now they are accessible only to one another
at a thousand feet. On sunless days they bask
in their obscurity. We, bemused
and rooted, observe this parade
of strange, muffled, self-loving creatures,
unnerving the dogs and flustering the swans
and talking to themselves and walking away from us
through the air, their faces hidden.

THE LAUNCH

When we float your blossom-poems downstream,
they are one with the current, they kiss earth
briefly in every cove.

WITH SEAMUS HEANEY IN MIND

1. The Poet's Death

On every continent the phones relay
your name as elegy, the calendars make way
across the hemispheres for your death day.

2. At the Graveside

We stand in a shy courtesy of loss.
A friend has set out without us, as he must,
on a long journey. No forwarding address.

3. Visiting the Grave

We visit your grave on weekdays, you who dressed
the ordinary weekday in its Sunday best
and the weekday heart of Sunday taking its rest.

STARLINGS

1. A Big Hand

A big hand for the starlings'
performance art.
For the electric minute
when the city releases its soul
as a gleaming shower,
and, charmed by the poetry of starlings,
everybody looks up.

2. Every Curve

Every curve is a learning curve.
The starlings disappear
behind a stand of winter trees.
They emerge with what may be a somber wisdom
or the password for spring.

3. Élite

Whatever the meaning of their fly-past,
the starlings are an élite,
their immaculate inner sanctum
cruising the skies.

4. Starlings at Play

There are more of them than we thought.
Consider the show of strength
when a thousand rise as one
from the stonework of a public building.
One lovely sweep deserves another.
To sit on the grass and stare is the best we can manage
as they pretend to crash *en masse*
into the municipal trees.

THE KINGFISHER

On the one occasion we saw a kingfisher,
his progress was royal.
He might have come up the river
to confirm the rumor of himself
and quicken our sense of wonder.
Surely he found our sleepy stream depressing.
No fish, no current, no oxbows,
not one decent meander.
Was it pity or indifference kept him posed
half the afternoon, long enough for a neighbor
with a camera to whirr-and-flash
a dozen tasteful close-ups. And that was that.
Suddenly we were tired of beauty and beauty of us.
As he aimed himself towards home,
there must have been moments
when he saw us as blocks of wood.
We too were fatigued by the speed of that arrow
into its jeweled future and the way evening
seemed to open as though it had held
for his expected passage, the day's final highlights.

AUTUMNAL

Take it or leave it, autumn is here again
to teach us about growing old gracefully.
Its smell is a special sap that is not a smell,
that's not snow in the air,
or the promise of sunshine,
or the fresh overtures of spring.
This month I stand again
in the middle of a park
while autumn conducts the year's first clear-out
leaving me dizzy, in spite of myself,
with its bleak wastefulness, its swirling gravity.

THE LAST LEAF IN THE GARDEN

I wish I had been there,
the garden stilled around the last
October leaf, nothing to hurry it,
nothing to slow it down.
The whole season has come to this:
a holding on so that the letting go
might seem to us like chance.
I wish I had been there
to see the wind carry the leaf beyond
the wall, if that is what happened,
winter, too, content to be late,
an elegant absence at the gate.

FUMS AND PORRINGERS

The men from the Folklore Commission
have come to collect
old words and sayings.
Children with four grandparents
come into their own.

It is the women, as always,
in whom the idioms survive.
We are proud to record
that our mother knows
about "fums" and "porringers."

We have never been so conscious
of ourselves, winning praise
from the strangers.
"Fums" and "porringers"
we hum under our breath.

My father, meanwhile goes back
to being "silent as the grave."

THE URBAN FOX

He carries the hunch of trespass
into suburban gardens,
directs a ten-second stare
that somehow makes the trespass ours.
He has the look of a raider
who has come to topple our wheelies
and nose through the garbage.
Sooner or later he will encounter the dogs.
He will not settle among us. He is dressed
for autumn in the woods and headed that way.

SCARECROW

I think of her day and night, the ragdoll
who won a prize for the lady of the house
in the Creative Arts competition at the Town Hall.
I hear that she lives in a cornfield further west
with an attractive, sewn-on smile
and a placard around her neck that says:
"Sisters Are Doing It for Themselves."
Has she heard of me? There are thirty sounds
for loneliness in the language of scarecrows.
We have fifty pangs for longing
that will never become words. We have patience and pathos
and bring to the fields an appetite for civic virtues.
We do poignancy better than anyone.

THE SUITCASE

It came to light in our attic,
in a corner we had thought all shadow.
Unpacking the newspaper lining
was like opening a small tomb full of dust.
After decades of railway platforms and luggage racks
and modest hotels, it had fetched up here.
We hadn't the heart to throw it on a skip
or consign it to the flames.
Best would be a suitcase museum,
redolent of journeys, the pain and excitement of moving on.
The newspaper established that they had packed it
in October 1939 and kept it at the ready for as long
as the century needed, as long as it takes
to become a refugee or fit a case-full of belongings
under one arm and start again. Whatever the story,
we eased the case back into its exact shadow
and left it, as a Brigid's cross is left behind the front door,
or a mezuzah on the doorpost, to bring blessings
on the house, to make something of its past ours.

AT A RAILWAY STATION, CALCUTTA

The two boys manoeuvre an old suitcase
down the side of a tip until
the bottom falls open. They make off with it
through the sidings between stationary trains.
Though scarred on one side, the case opens and closes
and seems to have been emptied of its former lives.
The boys will drag it to the camp outside the station
and fill it again, then, proud custodians,
hoist it onto the roof of the train.
There it begins life once more as a family centerpiece,
stained by the dust-plains in its journey,
unshaken by the tense delays at border checkpoints.
The elders rest against it, the children take turns
to clutch the handles, as though their project were to prevent
it from flying away in a slipstream of knickknacks,
blankets and miscellaneous belongings. When darkness
falls out of the sky, reluctantly they
put their heads down and hope for sleep.
Nothing all night but the roar of packed trains,
their restless patterns. By morning it is as if
a whole continent is sleeping off a huge transfusion.
Meanwhile, father's mother is now so small, her lower half lies curled
in the family suitcase that survived the Indian Mutiny.
It wears its history lightly, as everything does in time.

WINTER LANDSCAPE WITH SEARCHERS

I search for a field of unmarked graves
at the foot of a mountain. The winter leaves
and the random wind let nothing pass,
are taking a seminar on loss.

The wind is first to forget the dead,
the graves, wind-scoured, quick to fade
into bogs and beaches, bones interred
in the mountain beds of the disappeared.

The land is a patchwork of the deceased,
anonymous corners gone to seed,
from the decor of the family plot
to the famine grave and the cholera pit.

I fall in step as the searchers press
home in the dusk without success.
Winter rains begin to drown
remote, unconsecrated ground.

HE WAS THE EIGHTH TO GO MISSING

He was the eighth to go missing.
They find his body under fresh spring grass
and last season's rubble.
Hoisted with a kind of reverence,
he is slow-shouldered at last
along the main street of his home village.
The mourners have taken charge. They will go on
waiting because waiting
became the direction of their days.
They wait as though something singular
might yet be done with the ten lost years.
Their silence extends a passionate vigil,
a vast fidelity that may
last the rest of their lives.
The cortege halts at the graveside. The adults bow.
Schoolchildren duck forward to lay wreaths
of mountain heather on the wet clay.

BILLY ROBINSON'S KAWASAKI

For a while the ugliest sound in the world
was Billy Robinson's Kawasaki
ripping and tearing centuries of peace
in a field beyond the Plantation.
That field was becoming a dirt-track
where Billy cornered boldly with one knee
almost touching the ground. We, who rarely raised
our voices, listened with unease. Complaints were lost
on Billy, who stared at us eerily, through goggles
like the eyes of a different species.
An epic skid — the track was there to see —
broke both of Billy's legs. The bike stayed
upright, uttering its high-pitched snarl,
then head-butted a tree and was sold as scrap.
Peace in the land. Until Billy acquired a chainsaw.

ABANDONED GARDENS

Quiet as ivy, your footsteps, one by one,
in an abandoned garden.
You cannot breathe there without a sense of loss.
The weight of an abandoned garden waits for you
to be pressed into silence. Its graceful emptiness
contains the urge to subdue. Commanding ruin,
it never got used to losing the muted sounds
of adults and children, or decades of gardeners' voices
in the ivied gloom, their speech at an appropriate volume.
Just imagine the petulant fuss around your ankles
of Ruffles and Bouncer and Rupert, interred long since
in the cemetery for pets. Immediately
you want to leave. Immediately you know
that leaving may be the only option,
where weeds flourish and angels guard the gate.
Quiet as ivy your footsteps, one by one,
abandoning the garden.

SOME FARMYARD BUCKETS

The zinc buckets are having a get-together
in a corner of the yard. They are empty just now
with the peculiar emptiness of farm buckets
on day release.

The milk-carrier
holds a whiff of yesterday,
the turf bucket reeks of fums, but the meal bucket
is so fragrant you could fit it over your head and
breathe inside.

The slack-bucket is ringed
with a fine black grain. The swill-bucket has had
its sides licked clean, both inside and out.

This smaller one is lined
most days, with straw to keep the eggs intact.
Sometimes, the children, playing House, tuck in
an outraged gosling.

Here is the one we carried
to the well before the pipes were laid,
that never returned without a skim of seeds and insects.

A clutch of farmyard buckets, half-catching the light.
Beside them, fixed to a tap, the power hose
that will strike like a cloudburst,
that will drench and pummel them clean.

THE HATCHET

When we visit the County Museum, our first stop
is the glass case that exhibits the broken axe.
We call it "our hatchet." My father was clearing
a dunghill when it surfaced,
straight from the 16th century, when history in these parts
was taking a snooze. What, if anything,
did the axe signify? An end to rebellion?
Weaponry stored for the next rising, the one
that never happened? Or was it simply used to chop wood?
The axe gives nothing away, though now the star
of a postcard photograph. The glass case offers only
lights and ghostly refractions of ourselves.
There's a limit to what one artifact can recover
of the dead past. Nevertheless, our last stop is to buy
a postcard. The broken axe is in the family now,
like the rain barrel and the scarecrow.

CUSTODIANS

Among the custodians of the farm tonight,
the scarecrow we left out all winter
in the cornfield and the newly-minted snowman
in the back yard. If they touch freezing point
no one will know but themselves.
Could be they have an arrangement with the moon
that will let the thaw begin early.

The mists come up from the hollows. The weather vane is still.
In the byre a St. Brigid's Cross presides
over the sounds cattle make in their sleep.

THERE WILL BE A KNOCK

There will be a knock on the front door.
He will stand there twisting his hat, saying "Sorry, I'm late."
She checks the mail every day for his handwriting.
His room is packed with nine years
of birthday and Christmas gifts.
When asked why she does not move away
to a place with fewer painful memories, she replies,
"But what if he arrives on the doorstep
and we are gone? What will he do?"

WAKE IN PROGRESS

Somewhere to the left of my soul,
there is a wake in progress,
all day, every day.
Sometimes a crowd gathers,
sometimes there is no one
beside an empty coffin
but me, the chief mourner.
Somewhere to the right of my soul
I share a room with love and poetry
and the urge to be better than I am.
Grant me a fool's pardon, forgive me (or not)
my one enabling illusion, that
between the left of my soul and the right
I shall live forever.

SLEEPING AND FORGETTING

I had two lines in my head when I boarded the bus
for Queen's, but slept until jolted awake beyond House of Sport.
Forty minutes back to the bookstore. I caught the last poem
of Kate Newmann's reading.

I had fashioned two substantial lines about — what? —
when I fell asleep on a bench in the Waterworks park.
Not one pensive note in my pensive notebook
could help me recover either.

I had four cracking lines about death, but nodded off
in a corner of the bookstore. Now I write everything down
as it occurs, the words sluicing like insulin
through thirsty cells, challenging forgetfulness and sleep.

THE BOMB

Into my dream
comes a muffled figure from an amateur video,
darting through a supermarket to plant his bomb.
Is it a stroke or is it a heart attack?
He has caught me in the eye-slit of his balaclava.
He runs towards me with a calm intent.

THE SECURITY MAN

All through the sleety morning he keeps his body
close to the heater,
its oil-blue flame the flickering subdued essence
of his emptiest hours.

A screen on a low table is showing repeats
of yesterday's program,
stills of a wire cage outside of a building,
cement in barrels.

So long has he watched, those might be the wet pavements
of a different city,
the images come to his elbow with dripping raincoats
a kind of surprise,

and they, reflexively, submit themselves
to his ritual patting,
their eyes across his shoulders already fixed
on the empty tables.

And that's it for the moment. It has been a year
since he mustered suspicion.
They have not looked at him and he has gone back
to supplementing his pension.

CHAGALL'S GOATS

In Chagall's paintings
there are over 400 goats,
many of them smiling
at the edge of a village,
up for some crazy goat-craic.

If you close your eyes tonight
you will be at the mercy
of Chagall's ambivalent goats.
The one at the foot of the bed, for example,
is he a local good-time goat
or a sex-tourist from Sicily?

ARISTOTLE REACHES FERMANAGH

Somewhere in the fields around here
there was a hedge-school run by Master Doak,
its curriculum classical,
its pupils shouldering the school fees
in potatoes and turf.
During my father's lifetime there were still old men
who talked of their schooling:
"Master Kane broke us in on philosophy
with the book of the Harry Shuttle."

ROSARY

Your death in another country.
Birds restless on the wires:
breaking news.

Breaking news.
Birds restless on the wires.
Your death in another country.

Your death in another country.
Breaking news.
Birds restless on the wircs.

Birds restless on the wires.
Breaking news.
Your death in another country.

RAINS

The valley rains are a drifting, fine spray.
In half a minute or less you are wet through.
The rain from the hills brings down on you
the full weight of its attention.
Give me the brisk soul-wash of the valley rains
when the spirit wants lifting.
Give me the rain from the hills, so that I am faced,
over and over, with its candid, questioning fall.

PULSE

Hands cupped,
I take the water's pulse
halfway
between the spout
and the rain barrel.

THE RAIN BARREL

1. Prologue

It was so much a family emblem,
like the axe-head found in the dunghill,
or the scarecrow set at the highest
point on the farm, playfully attired
in Grandad Joe's old clothing. You could imagine
the rain barrel soaked in experience, shaped elsewhere,
in another country, perhaps. Did it ring sturdily
in the making? Did it have time
to grieve for the forest? I picture it left out in the rain,
a short apprenticeship, now snatch it
from memory, restore it to its place
between the four square-eyed front windows.
Rain comes shimmering in over the hills.
At home in a rain-weighty climate
the barrel stands ready for its first shower.

2. We Acquire the Rain Barrel

We are the first in the parish to own a rain barrel.
Pagan as any thorn,
it will brook no nonsense.
It is like something orphaned in a field,
and, when empty, smells like a hip-flask.

Fresh duties now, all of them in the realm of water.
We install it the same day.
The first drip from the spout
is a kind of baptism.

3. Notes Towards a Portrait of the Rain Barrel

It is motionless,
but never inert. In all weathers
it brings to the front of the house
the nuances of keeping still
dynamically. Its life, lived in the open,
garners small excitements:
the drowned fieldmouse,
the dead wasp that must have floated
a week before anyone noticed,
the day it got hammered by hailstones.

4. A Busy Life

I imagined it as keeper of the thunder.
It took the weightlessness
of nameless flies, diaphanous midges,
a frog caught on the hop and dropped
as from a diving board,
then fished out in a colander,
dead insects, sycamore seeds, the sun and moon,
in all their phases. Something inviolable
outshone the wear and tear. Its inaudible duets
with the wind and rain trickled through our sleep,
notes towards an elegy
for rain barrels.

5. The Rain Barrel in the Snow

It is snowing into the rain barrel's
dark-watered maw. The barrel
feeds like a whale on plankton.
By the time it has stopped snowing,
the level will have risen an inch or two.
The barrel is developing an urge to spill over.

6. In the Family

How long has the rain barrel been in the family?
You could have drowned in it as quickly
as in a slurry-tank or a lint-hole,
yet your childhood's growth was measured
against the rusty iron hoops.

7. Two Old Warriors

Two old warriors, the rain barrel and my father,
sit with their backs to the wall,
one receiving daily the gift of water,
the other struggling to accept the gifts of air.

8. Still Life

The rain barrel carries
a lid of thick ice
into the morning.
We chip at it with a hammer
until it floats,
then set it aside
like a delicate, damaged bowl.
Snotters of ice hang
from the spout. The rain barrel
is a still life of itself
until the freeze relents
and sanctions its release.

9. Lost Lives

Idle imaginings of the life it might enjoy
in another existence;
muscle man, weight lifter, bouncer,
the strongman in a circus,
the guardian of a mountain pass,
a sculpture in a secluded sculpture garden:
Torso With Gravitas.

10. Romance

Aunt Annie brought the barrel a present once,
a cherry blossom beaten by the rain
into bruised glory. It was worse
than an arranged marriage.
The blossom, though floating gamely,
succumbed at last
to a bedraggled burial at sea.

11. Interlude, with Girls

Alive to the special properties
of fresh rain water, the girls,
from time to time, immerse their heads.
Almost immediately they re-emerge,
spluttering and shaking themselves
like dogs under a hose.
Now would be the very time, if we had the skills,
to paint on a vaudeville moustache,
a Brylcreemed head, some extravagant sideburns.
But this morning the barrel belongs to the girls,
scalps soaking, water in their eyes,
though it seems oblivious
of the Parade of the Turbanned Heads.
Serenity itself, it takes spillage in its stride,
builds again slowly from the bottom.

12. The Rain Barrel and the Full Moon

In winter the full moon
takes a shine to the rain barrel,
offering its face for reflection.
The barrel keeps putting on weight
or so it seems
until the little droughts of summer
empty it again to the first hoop.

13. Photograph, with Rain Barrel

So strong does the rain barrel look
on the day of the funeral
that it might be carrying
clay as well as water.
Amid all the talk
of imminent heavy rain,
it maintains the judicious silence
for which rain barrels are famous.
Somebody points a camera,
the window fills
with mourners' faces
taken by surprise.
Their impulse to duck and dodge
has cleared a path
back to that squat presence.
We stare into the space
where our father's chair
is no longer part of the prospect.

14. The Rain Barrel and the Sparrows

The smallest birds are among the heaviest drinkers.
They balance on the rim and refuel
with dainty jabs. What do they make of their reflections,
the lurking, murderous intent of the farmyard cats?

It never comes to bloodshed. Worse by far
the hopeless pecking at a plate of ice
by winter sparrows. We dump
the fridge-cold innards, stir the depths
with a broom from the outhouse. Their local
serving free drink again,
the parish sparrows return in ones and twos.

15. Another Use for a Rain Barrel

Benny McMulkin is shooting
off his mouth again: next minute
we have the little runt by the ankles
over the rain barrel, his head
touching the water.
"Make a wish, Benny," we taunt
between dunkings. We shake him
till every coin in his pockets
sinks to the bottom,
carrying with it
Benny's silent wishes.

16. Lightning and the Rain Barrel

What might lightning mean to a rain barrel?
Lightning might be its mother and father,
its distant relatives, its estranged wife, its god,
or, when it strikes at night,
the ache in the darkness of everything
for let there be light.

17. Some Other Duties for a Rain Barrel

One year there was a surplus of apples
and the rain barrel half-filled
like the one in *Treasure Island*.
We christened the apples "big knobblies,"
ate from the barrel every time we passed
and checked for stowaways.
When Fermanagh got through the first round
of the Championship, we flew a green flag
from the top of the barrel and exchanged cheers
with flag waving cars on the main road.
Mostly the barrel was king of its own country,
a benign dictatorship, built into the house
and into our lives.

18. The Butt

Old age catches up as links and shrinkage
and the hoops loosen.
At last it is taken away on a tractor
to be dismantled. Two dependable buckets sit in place
where the spout goes on processing
rainfall straight from the clouds.

The replacement, a barrel half the size,
does not command half the respect.
We christen it the Butt.

WHEN SHE DIED, THINKING OF HIM

When she died, thinking of him,
his body had not been found.
His was the blank stone
already in place
at the center of the plot
next to his father's.
On Cemetery Sunday,
his father tended one empty grave.
Soon there will be no one alive
who knows where the body is,
whether on its back or face down,
whether rooted in mountain or bog,
or bound in plastic at the bottom of a lake.
The chances are he will be lost forever
and the blank stone in the middle
will fall to neglect under a soft moss
of forgetfulness, the ground still seeded
with the unfound, the undiscovered, the disappeared.

NO CLOSURE

Someday perhaps there will be no graves
or memory of graves on the mountain.
The empty plots will return to the wilderness,
their business now entirely with the seasons
and the unpredictable sky. History there will be
the stiff nodding of bog cotton, wind on stone,
a grouse rising and settling without fear.

RAIN FLOWERS

If I could design a flower
for these fields, it would be a plain
blossom, a flower of mist and rain,
stirred into life by the lightest shower.

Picture a rare species planted in line,
clear of all shelter, sharing dreams of Spain
with their friends the mud-flowers. As they drink the rain,
every drop is changed to an earth-dark wine.

GRACE BEFORE MEALS

The wrens, having gauged the exact
springiness of the tall, bearded grasses,
ride them to within an inch of the ground
and begin feeding. Impeccable.

THE DOGS

Forgotten, the names
of the two dogs we lost
to the main road.
In memory they are one.

Today, in memory, I take them for a run
in the Waterworks park,
the air clamorous
with the language of dogs' names.

BEYOND THE WALLS

1. By the River

Long summer days,
the deft shimmy of midges
tormenting cattle.

2. Miss Brightly

Miss Brightly on her pony and trap
elegantly skirting potholes
on the avenue to the castle.

3. The Peacock

The fantail extravaganza
of the castle peacock
puts the vintage car rally in the shade.

4. Souvenir

Visitors stop to take photographs:
Colonel Armstrong's black stallion,
parading his cock round the paddock.

THE GREY SQUIRREL

Lovely, genocidal squirrel,
cuddliest of mass murderers,
so at home in the woods,
you know where the mass graves lie.

SHARING BEDS

After his death,
she continued to sleep in their bed
and when she tended his grave
it was her own grave also she tended.

THE PARENTS WAIT

Whatever waiting is,
the day we stop,
something vast as
an immeasurable ocean
will begin to recede.
We will know
that time is thoughtless
and has no concept of loss,
that even with others
we must bear this knowledge,
daily and endlessly,
into the faceless, curled future.

PARENTS

I never saw them laugh together
or exchange angry words.
Their silence fed the hundred silences
between home and the mountains.

LESSONS

How to unlock that silence.
As I pictured it, we would set them
face to face in front of the fire.
They would be allowed one word each,
the other's Christian name.
Even this, the first lesson,
would be too much, too quickly,
but it seemed best
that they had no time to think.
Instructed to touch,
they must immediately
achieve hand-on-hand
or hand-on-arm contact.
This, the second lesson, would also be
too late, the years so deep
that no reversal would be enough,
the patterns so set they had comfortably
become the life between —
in the hayfield, across the hearth, together at prayer —
were not to be fathomed
or tampered with. Chastened, what could we
do but take from them
our first and last lesson:
to let that silence be.

VISITORS, 4 A.M.

Homeless in the dark,
the night's surfers and blow-ins
stagger towards my light,
then sheer off through a vast elsewhere
on papery, vagabond wings.

THE ROUNDABOUT

The roundabout at the top of the village street
signposts the road to the capital.
The name of the capital has disappeared under white paint
and the top of the sign has been bent double,
almost to breaking point, directing you back
up the village street. How slow we are to accept change.

ALL HE REMEMBERED

He claimed that all he remembered of the war
was how, the week the blackout ended,
the evening bus blazed between wet hedgerows,
an ark of light.

OUR WOODS WERE FRIENDLY

Our woods were friendly.
The warty churl with the gun
was neither soft in the head
nor the woodcutter's bastard son.
Nobody disappeared.
Sometimes, just for fun,
we sowed a trail of breadcrumbs
and followed it home.

THE TWO TREES

They faced each other on a country road
like an old couple, dry-skinned and durable,
the forgotten grandparents of the parish.
They had stood there for decades and nobody tendered
an arm or offered a chair. Finally a storm-vandal
from the Atlantic blew them away. Nothing left
but two hollow teeth in the undergrowth.

THAW

The wind has shut down. Even the winter sun
is in accord with the hundred-and-one tunes
of the plantation trees dripping in unison.

RUNNING WATER

Somebody threw a switch and water bloomed
in the new kitchen sink and the modest tap in the yard.
The little pipes filled underground, veining the farms.

Never again the walk from the well in the woods.
Sensing the gift of its first stillness restored,
it settles itself among ferns and floating leaves.

AFTER FERNANDO PESSOA

Everything in the universe is beyond belief
but I reach out daily in the act of believing.
O my fugitive unbelief,
let my reaching out
be always
to what is beyond belief.

ACKNOWLEDGMENTS

Acknowledgments are due to the editors of the following magazines and newspapers in which some of these poems first appeared: *Archipelago*, *Arís*, *The Cavehill Campaigner*, *Reading the Future: New Writing from Ireland* (ed. Alan Hayes), *The Irish Times*, *The New Yorker*, *Poetry Ireland Review*, *Poetry Review*, *Reading Ireland*, and *The Tangerine*. A number of poems were broadcast on BBC Radio Ulster, BBC Radio 4 and Radio Éireann.

"The Secondhand Bookshop" was published in *Happy Browsing: An Anthology in Praise of Bookfinders*, assembled as a tribute to Mary Denvir when the bookshop closed in 2018.

"Abandoned Gardens," "Autumnal," "Saying Goodbye to the Family," and "The Poets" were published in *7 Poets, 7 Poems*, a limited edition of fifty copies, edited by John Brown, for the Fenderesky Gallery, 2018.

"At the Graveside" and "Visiting the Grave" from "With Seamus Heaney in Mind" appeared as separate poems in my collection *The Darkness of Snow* (2017).

"Fums and Porringers" will feature in a forthcoming exhibition of the National Folklore Collection of Ireland.

NOTES

"Fums and Porringers": "Fums" is the term used in Fermanagh to describe the inferior turf found on the surface of bogland. A "porringer" is defined in the *Concise Oxford Dictionary* as "a small basin from which children eat soup."

"Aristotle Reaches Fermanagh": This poem is based on an anecdote by the Fermanagh musician and singer Paddy Tunney in his memoir *The Stone Fiddle* (1979).